G000165713

Progressive
ROCK GUITAR LICKS

by
Brett Duncan

Visit our Website
www.learntoplaymusic.com

The Progressive Series of Music Instruction Books, CDs, and DVDs

CD TRACK LISTING

1	Tuning Notes	15	Lesson 11 Ex 62-65
2	Lesson 1 Ex 1-5	16	Lesson 12 Ex 66-71
3	Lesson 2 Ex 6-11	17	Solo 3 - Two's Company
4	Lesson 3 Ex 12-18	18	Ex 72-73
5	Lesson 4 Ex 19-25	19	Lesson 13 Ex 74-78
6	Solo 1 - One for the Road	20	Lesson 14 Ex 79-83
7	Lesson 5 Ex 26-32	21	Lesson 15 Ex 84-88
8	Lesson 6 Ex 33-39	22	Solo 4 - The Hat Trick
9	Lesson 7 Ex 40-43	23	Ex 89-90
10	Lesson 8 Ex 44-48	24	Lesson 16 Ex 91-94
11	Solo 2 - All For One and One For All	25	Lesson 17 Ex 95-100
12	Ex 49-50	26	Solo 5 - The Fouth Dimension
13	Lesson 9 Ex 51-55	27	Ex 101-102
14	Lesson 10 Ex 56-61	28	Lesson 18 Ex 103-106
		27	Solo 6 - The Penthathlon

PROGRESSIVE ROCK GUITAR LICKS
I.S.B.N. 0 947183 74 4
Order Code: CP-18374

Acknowledgments
Cover Photograph: Phil Martin
Photographs: Phil Martin

For more information on this series contact;
L.T.P. Publishing Pty Ltd
email: info@learntoplaymusic.com
or visit our website;
www.learntoplaymusic.com

COPYRIGHT CONDITIONS
No part of this product can be reproduced in any
form without the written consent of the publishers.
© 2004 L.T.P. Publishing Pty Ltd

Contents

Contents (cont)

Introduction

Progressive Rock Guitar Licks incorporates the many different techniques, scales and patterns used in modern styles of Rock Guitar. This book may be used by itself or as a useful supplement to *Progressive Rock Guitar Technique* which discusses in more detail the techniques and scales used in this book.

The licks throughout the book are based upon licks employed by the world's best Rock guitarists and are progressively set out in order of difficulty to assist Rock guitar players of all levels.

It will be helpful to already have a basic knowledge of guitar before starting this book. (See *Progressive Rock Guitar Method* and *Progressive Rock Guitar Technique* by Brett Duncan). Beginners of Rock guitar will be able to start with the first section and progressively work through this book while more experienced players will be able to further develop their knowledge of this style.

There are five sections throughout the book, each dealing with one of the five popular Rock guitar patterns which are used on the fretboard. The final section is a summary of all the patterns and keys used throughout this book.

The licks in each section are examples of how each pattern may be used, and how various techniques can be applied to each pattern. At the end of each section is a Rock guitar solo, which fully shows how the licks and techniques learnt throughout each section can be used to create a Rock guitar solo.

It is also recommended to work through this book in association with the accompanying recording which will allow you to hear how all the licks and solos should sound. You will also be able to practice along with backing tracks, giving you the opportunity to create your own solos.

Good Luck and have fun,

Brett Duncan

Other Progressive Rock Guitar Books:

Progressive Rock Guitar Method
FOR BEGINNING ROCK GUITARISTS

A comprehensive, lesson by lesson introduction to Rock Guitar. Covers in detail the basics of rhythm and lead guitar with over 50 examples and progressions. Clearly notated in music and tablature.

Progressive Rock Guitar Technique
FOR INTERMEDIATE ROCK GUITARISTS

A comprehensive, easy to follow guide, covering all aspects of Rock Guitar. Includes basic chords, bar chords, rhythm patterns lead guitar scales and techniques used by the world's best Rock Guitarists. Clearly notated in music and tablature.

Scale Diagrams Used In This Book

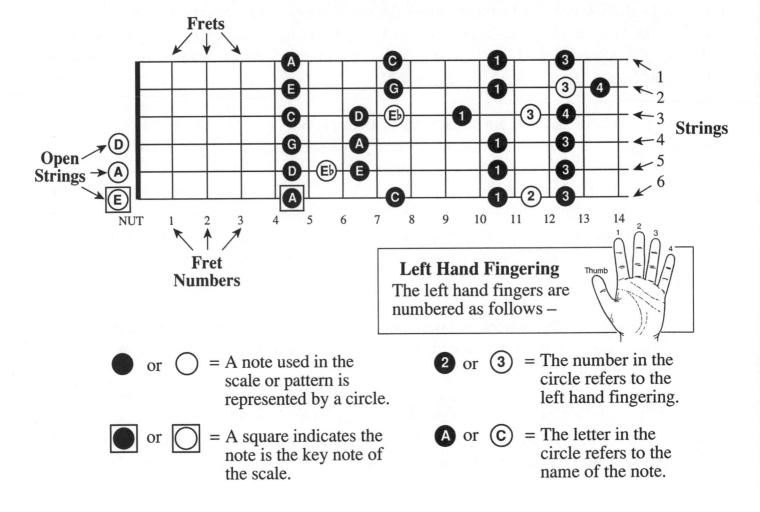

● or ○ = A note used in the scale or pattern is represented by a circle.

▣ or ☐ = A square indicates the note is the key note of the scale.

❷ or ③ = The number in the circle refers to the left hand fingering.

Ⓐ or Ⓒ = The letter in the circle refers to the name of the note.

Notation

This book uses standard music notation and tablature notation. If you cannot read music notes use the tab written below the music. Music readers will need to look at the tab to see what technique is being used to play certain notes (e.g. hammer, slide etc.)

Tablature

Tablature is a method of indicating the position of notes on the fretboard. There are six "tab" lines each representing one of the six strings on the guitar:

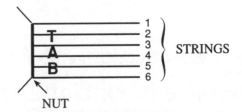

When a number is placed on one of the lines, it indicates the fret location of a note. e.g.

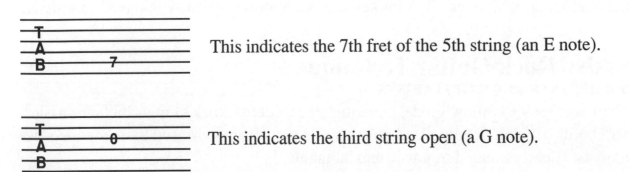

This indicates the 7th fret of the 5th string (an E note).

This indicates the third string open (a G note).

Tablature Symbols Used In This Book

The Hammer

A curved line and the letter H indicates a hammer. The first note is played but the second note is produced by hammering on the left hand finger which plays the second note.

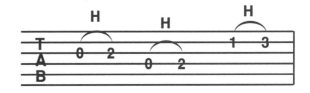

The Pull-Off

A curved line and the letter P indicates a pull-off. The first note is played but the second note is produced by pulling off the finger which is playing the first note.

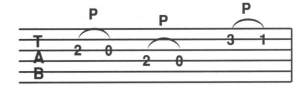

The Slide

The letter S and a straight line represents a slide. If the line comes from below the number, slide from a lower fret but if the line is above the number, slide from a higher fret. The third example on the right shows the desired fret to slide from.

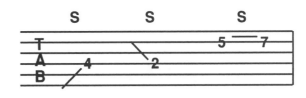

The Bend

The letter B and a curved line represents a bend. The note is played by the left hand finger which bends the string (from the note indicated in the tab).

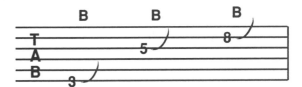

The Release Bend

A curved line on the top left hand side of the number and the letter R will indicate a release bend. The technique involves bending the note indicated with the left hand, plucking the string whilst bent, then returning the string to its normal position. The release bend creates a drop in pitch from a higher note to a lower note.

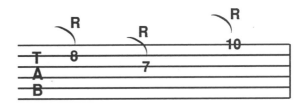

Vibrato

A wavy line shown above the tablature indicates when vibrato is used. Vibrato is controlled with the left hand finger which is fretting the note. As the finger frets the note, move the string rapidly back and forth in the direction of the adjacent strings.

Double-Note Licks

The symbol ⌐─┐ is used in the tablature to show two notes are sustained together when using a double-note lick. This time a note is bent, and whilst the note is sustaining, another note is played with a different finger, causing both notes to ring together.

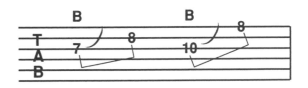

SECTION 1

Rock Guitar Licks
Pattern One

Pattern One

The first set of licks will be based upon the Minor Pentatonic scale within pattern one. This is the most popular pattern used in modern lead guitar styles. The pattern is movable, i.e. it can be played in different keys by changing its location on the fretboard. The diagram below shows pattern one in the key of G. Notice that the scale begins on the third fret of the sixth string (a G note).

Pattern One - Minor Pentatonic Scale

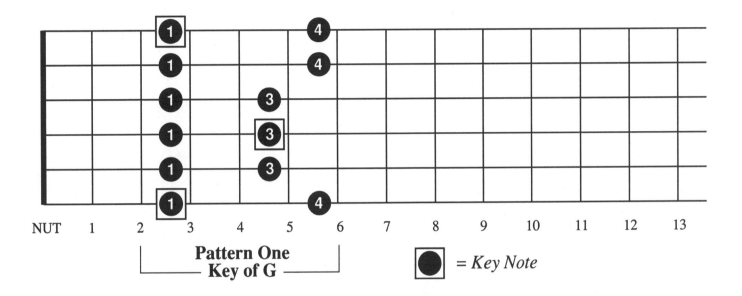

If you need to play this pattern in a different key, move the entire pattern up or down the fretboard to the desired fret. The first note in the pattern (on the sixth string) will indicate the key the scale is in. For example, if you want to play in the key of F, begin the pattern on the first fret of the sixth string (an F note). If you wish to play in the key of C, then begin the pattern on the eighth fret of the sixth string (a C note). Therefore the note on the sixth string will determine the key.

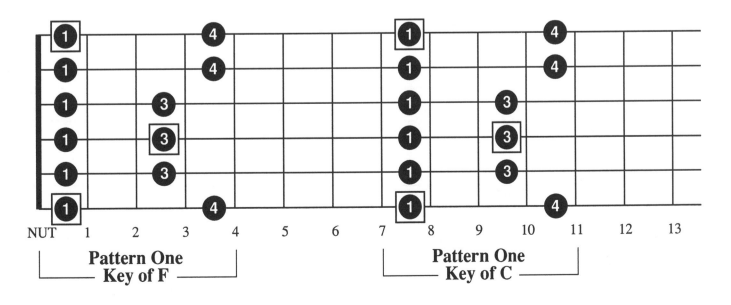

Lesson 1
Pattern One – Basic Examples

Example 1

The first example begins on the lowest note in pattern one and ascends up the scale to the highest note in the pattern. All the examples are given in the key of G, therefore beginning on the third fret of the sixth string. This example is played in quarter note rhythm. This means a note is played on every beat of the bar.

On the recording there are four drum beats to introduce this example. Listen carefully and play along with the recording.

The symbol **V** indicates that each note is played with a down stroke of the pick.

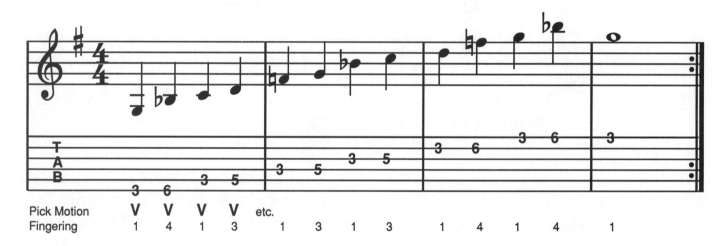

| Pick Motion | V V V V etc. | | | |
| Fingering | 1 4 1 3 | 1 3 1 3 | 1 4 1 4 | 1 |

Example 2

The second example descends from the highest note in the pattern to the lowest note in the pattern. Once again, listen to the recording carefully and play along.

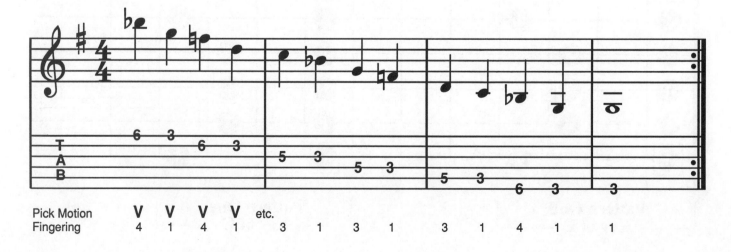

| Pick Motion | V V V V etc. | | | |
| Fingering | 4 1 4 1 | 3 1 3 1 | 3 1 4 1 | 1 |

Example 3

The next example is an eighth note exercise, meaning two notes will be played every beat, a total of eight notes to a bar. This example is counted "1 and 2 and 3 and 4 and", written "1 + 2 + 3 + 4 +". Two right hand picking variations have been given. Both variations should be practiced until the exercise is even and smooth. The symbol ∧ represents that the right hand uses an up stroke to play the note.

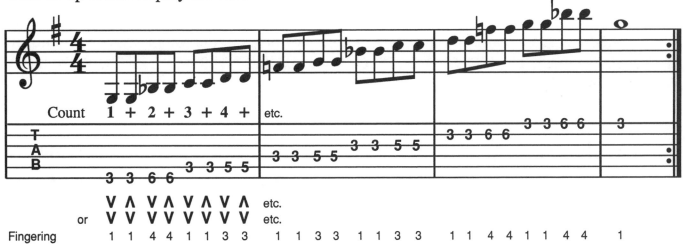

Example 4

Example four is similar to Example three but descends from the highest note in the pattern to the lowest note.

Example 5

The final example in this lesson ascends and descends pattern one using an eighth note rhythm.

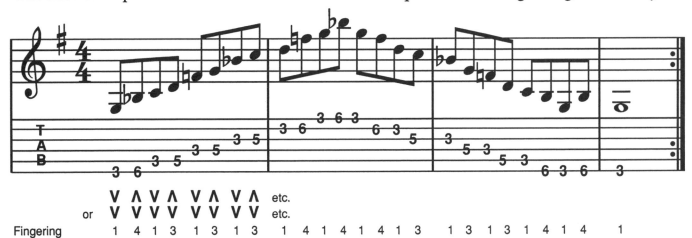

Lesson 2
Pattern One – Key of G

The next set of licks are in the key of G and are played within pattern one. Before tackling the following licks it will be helpful to have a basic knowledge of the Minor Pentatonic scale. The Minor Pentatonic scale consists of the 1 - ♭3 - 4 - 5 - ♭7 notes of the Major scale. The notes in the G Major scale are G A B C D E F♯ G. If we take the 1 - ♭3 - 4 - 5 - ♭7 notes of the G major scale we will end up with the notes G B♭ C D F.

6 G Major Scale

G A B C D E F♯ G

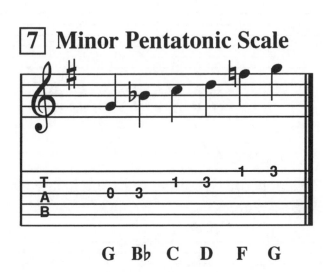

7 Minor Pentatonic Scale

G B♭ C D F G

Fretboard Position

Pattern one in the key of G begins on the third fret of the sixth string. The diagram below displays the exact position of pattern one in the key of G. The key note (G) is indicated by a square. Attention should be given to the other notes in the pattern (B♭ C D and F) which as discussed above are the other notes in the G Minor Pentatonic scale.

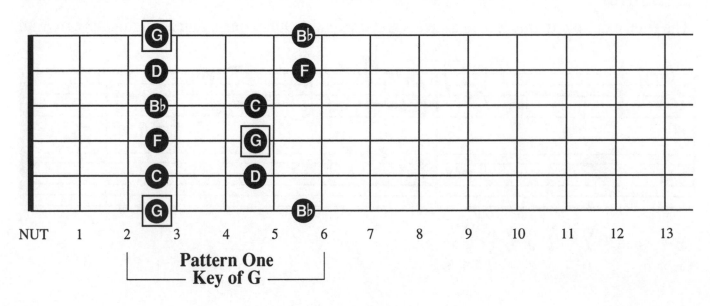

Licks 8 – 11 are in the key of G and played within pattern one.

Lesson 3
Pattern One – Key of A

The next set of licks are in the key of A Major. As with the previous lesson, look at the construction of the A Minor Pentatonic scale. To construct the A Minor Pentatonic scale the 1 - ♭3 - 4 - 5 - ♭7 notes of the A Major scale are needed. The notes in the A Major scale are A B C♯ D E F♯ G♯ A. If the 1 - ♭3 - 4 - 5 - ♭7 notes are taken from this scale, the notes A C D E and G are formed.

12 A Major Scale

A B C♯ D E F♯ G♯ A

13 A Minor Pentatonic Scale

A C D E G A

Fretboard Position

Pattern one in the key of A begins on the fifth fret of the sixth string (an A note). The pattern is made up of the notes A C D E and G, being the notes in the A Minor Pentatonic scale.

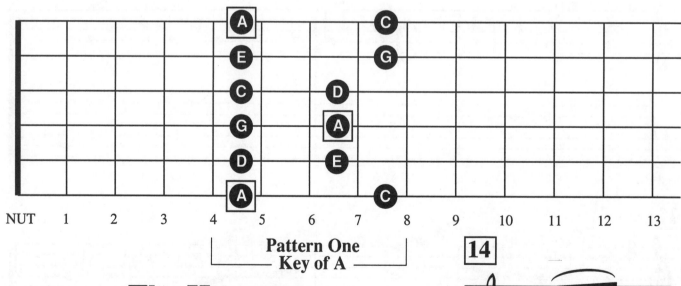

The Hammer

Licks 15 - 18 introduce the hammer between two notes. The first note is played, but the second note is produced by hammering on the left hand finger which plays the second note. The letter H and a curved line will indicate when a hammer is used. The following example shows a hammer from the fifth fret to the seventh fret on the fourth string.

14

Fingering   1   3

Licks 15 – 18 are in the key of A and are played within pattern one.

Lesson 4
Pattern One – Key of C

As with the previous keys discussed, the C Minor Pentatonic scale is also constructed from the C Major scale. The notes in the C Major scale are C D E F G A B C. The 1 - ♭3 - 4 - 5 - ♭7 notes taken from this scale are C E♭ F G B♭.

19 **C Major Scale**

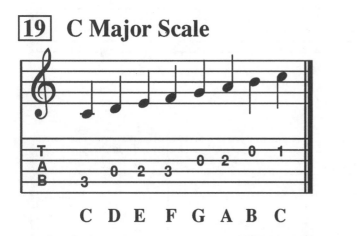

C D E F G A B C

20 **C Minor Pentatonic Scale**

C E♭ F G B♭ C

Fretboard Position

Pattern one in the key of C begins on the eighth fret of the sixth string (a C note). The pattern is made up of the notes C E♭ F G B♭, being the notes in the C Minor Pentatonic scale.

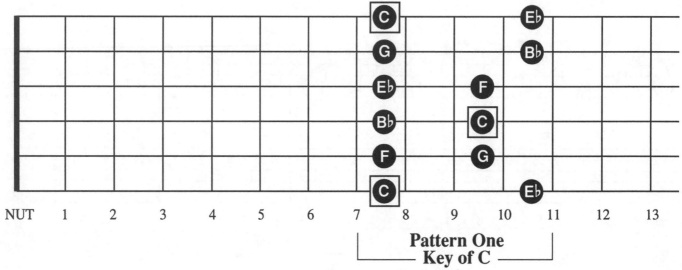

The Pull-off

Licks 22 - 25 introduce the pull-off. A curved line and the letter P indicates a pull-off. The first note is played but the second note is produced by pulling off the finger which is playing the first note. The following example shows a pull-off from the tenth fret to the eighth fret on the fourth string.

21

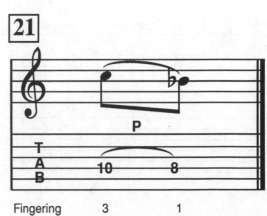

Fingering   3   1

Licks 22 – 25 are in the key of C and are played within pattern one.

Rock Guitar Solo 1
One For The Road

This first solo is played in the key of C and is played within pattern one. Pattern one in the key of C is positioned between the eighth and eleventh frets as explained in Lesson 4. The solo is made up of licks similar to the ones which have appeared in previous lessons.

The chord progression chosen for this solo is an eight bar rock progression in the key of C. As the chord progression changes through the chords, it will not be necessary to change the position of the pattern. This shows that the C Minor Pentatonic scale can be played over the C Major, F Major and G Major chords.

Eight Bar Rock Progression in C

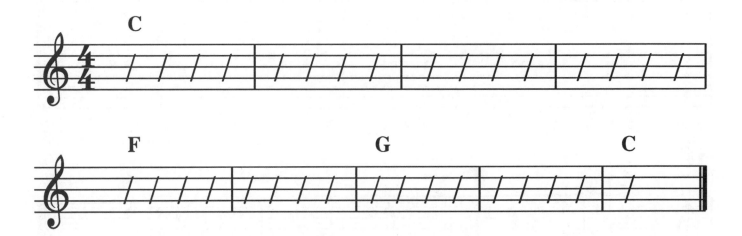

One For The Road – Analysis

- The hammer has been used throughout this solo. This technique was featured in Lesson 3.

- The other technique used in this solo is the pull-off which was introduced in Lesson 4.

Playing Along With The Cassette or CD

All the solos in this book have been recorded in stereo. This allows you to practice the solo in three different ways.

Firstly, by having the balance control on your stereo fully to the left, you will only hear the lead guitar by itself, giving you the opportunity to hear the solo clearly. With the balance control in the middle, you can play along with all the instruments thus hearing how the solo fits in with the backing music. Finally, practice with the balance control fully to the right and try playing the solo along with the rest of the band.

One For The Road

Lesson 5
Pattern One – Key of E

Lesson Five uses pattern one in the key of E. The notes in the E Minor Pentatonic scale are E G A B and D. These notes have been obtained from the E Major scale which consists of the notes E F♯ G♯ A B C♯ D♯ E.

26 **E Major Scale**

E F♯ G♯ A B C♯ D♯ E

27 **E Minor Pentatonic Scale**

E G A B D E

Fretboard Position

Pattern one in the key of E can be played in the open position as well as the twelfth fret position. The patterns are made up of the notes E G A B D, being the notes in the E Minor Pentatonic scale.

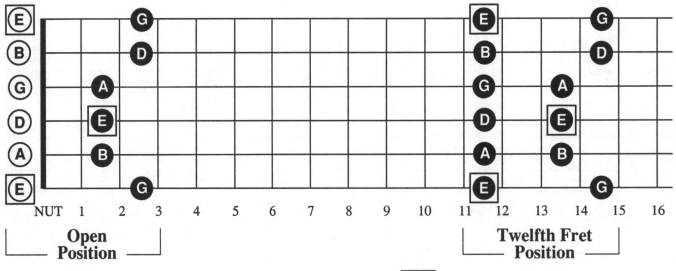

The Slide

Licks 29 - 32 introduce the slide. The letter S and a straight line represents a slide. If the line comes from below the number, slide from a lower fret, but if the line is above the number, slide from a higher fret. The third example shown indicates exactly which fret to slide from.

28

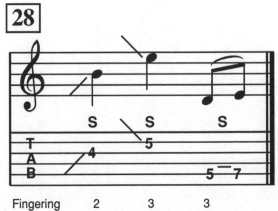

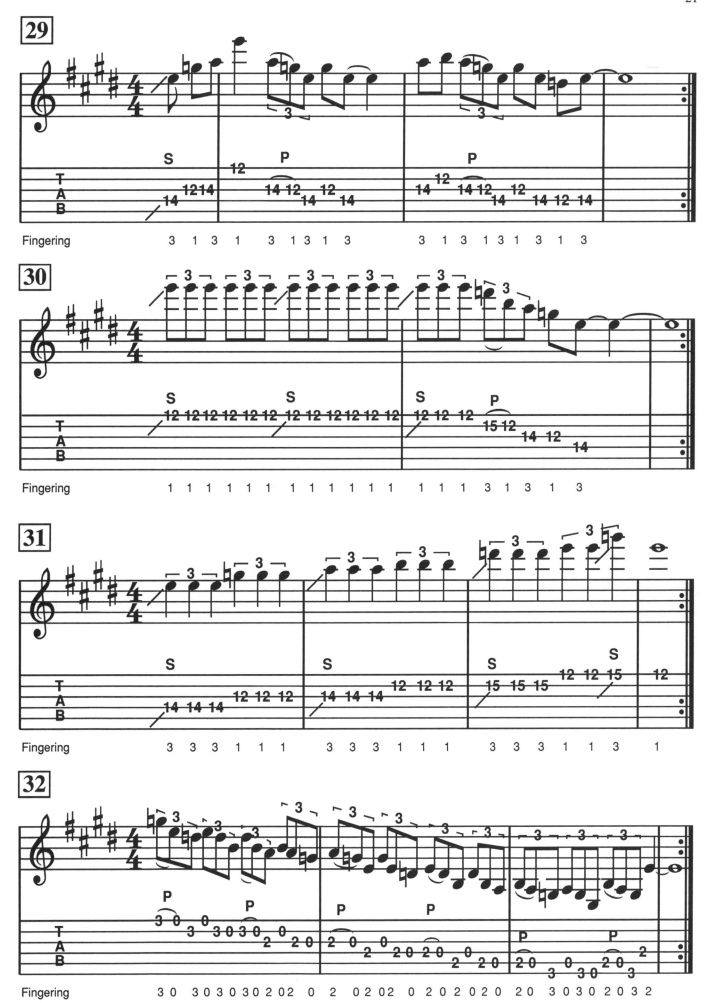

Lesson 6
Pattern One – Key of D

The next key featured will be the key of D. The construction of the D Minor Pentatonic scale is as previously discussed in earlier lessons. The 1 - ♭3 - 4 - 5 - ♭7 notes of the D Major scale will form the D Minor Pentatonic scale. The notes in the D Major scale are D E F♯ G A B C♯ D. After the alteration has been made to this scale, the notes D F G A and C form the D Minor Pentatonic scale.

33 D Major Scale

D E F♯ G A B C♯ D

34 D Minor Pentatonic Scale

D F G A C D

Fretboard Position

Pattern one in the key of D begins on the tenth fret of the sixth string. The pattern, in this position, consists of the notes D F G A and C, which as mentioned above are the notes in the D Minor Pentatonic scale.

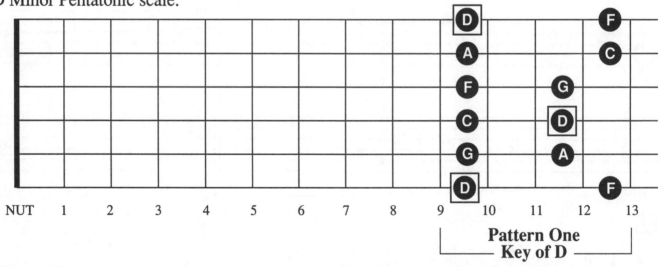

Pattern One
Key of D

The Bend

Licks 36 - 39 introduce the bend. The letter B and a curved line represents a bend. The note is played by the left hand finger which bends the string (from the note indicated in the tab). The example below shows a bend on the twelfth fret of the third string.

35

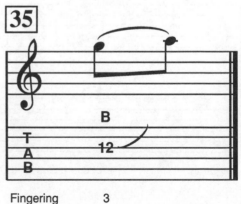

Fingering   3

Lesson 7
Pattern One - The Blues Scale

The scale which has been used in previous lessons was the Minor Pentatonic scale. By adding an extra note to the minor pentatonic scale a blues scale is formed. The extra note which is added is the flattened fifth note of the Major scale. The example below shows the construction of the C Blues scale.

C Major scale	C	D	E	F	G	A	B	C
	1	2	3	4	5	6	7	8

C Minor Pentatonic	C	E♭	F	G	B♭	C
	1	♭3	4	5	♭7	8

C Blues scale	C	E♭	F	G♭	G	B♭	C
	1	♭3	4	♭5	5	♭7	8

The Blues Scale Pattern

To incorporate this extra note into pattern one, add the notes on the third and fifth strings as indicated by the diagram below. When using this extra note, you are in effect playing a blues scale. The example shown below is in the key of G. The notes in the G blues scale are G B♭ C D♭ D and F. This is the same as the G Minor Pentatonic scale, except the flattened fifth note of the Major scale has been added (a D♭ note).

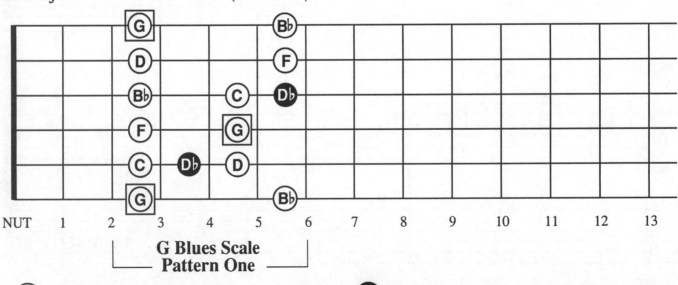

G Blues Scale
Pattern One

○ = Minor Pentatonic scale – Pattern One   ● = added note to complete Blues scale

The following licks are played using the 'E' blues scale.

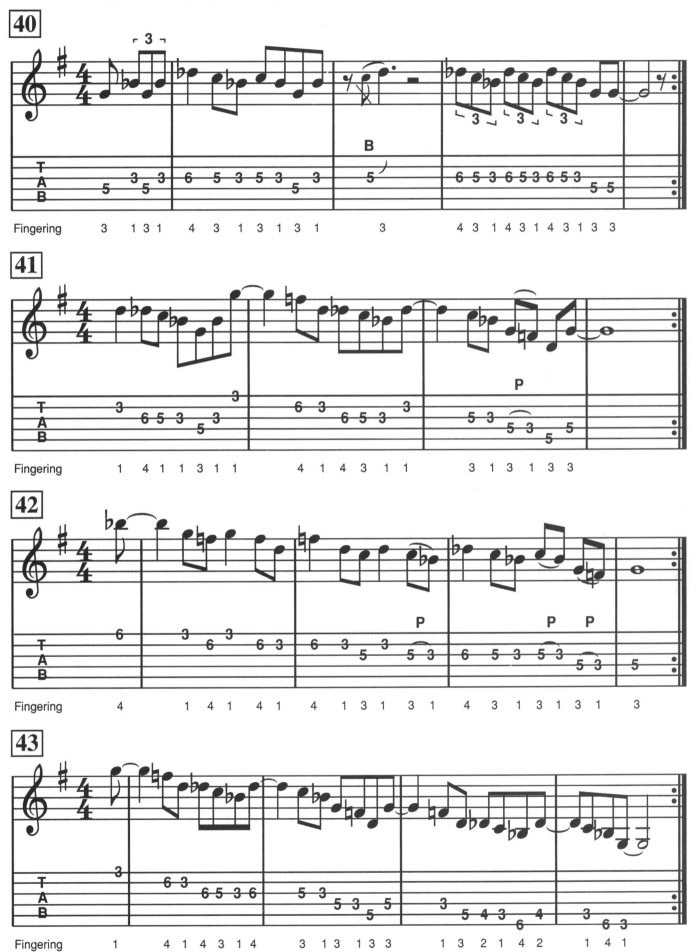

Lesson 8
Pattern One – Double Note Licks

The next set of licks are still played within pattern one, but introduce the use of double note licks. A double note lick is when two notes within the pattern are played together.

Example 44

The first example below is played in the key of A. The two notes on the fifth fret are played with the first finger of the left hand.

Fingering

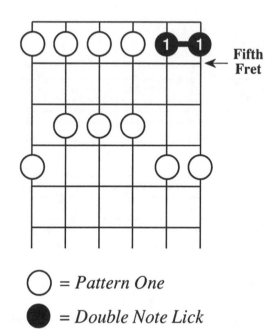

← Fifth Fret

○ = *Pattern One*

● = *Double Note Lick*

Example 45

The second example in this lesson introduces a double-note lick played on the eighth fret. These notes may be played with either the third or fourth finger.

Fingering

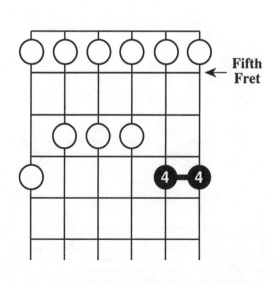

← Fifth Fret

Example 46

The next example shows two more double-note licks found on the second and third strings. You may notice an extra note has been added to the pattern on the second string. This extra note is the sixth note of the Major scale. The two notes played together on the fifth fret are played with the first finger. The notes on the seventh fret are played with the third finger.

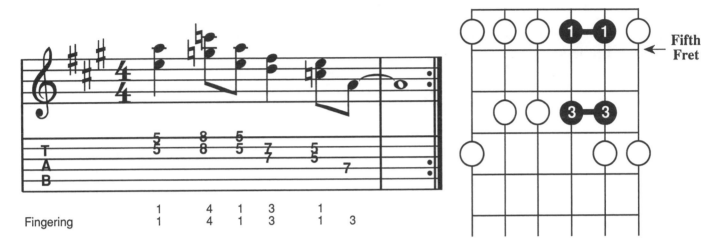

Fingering
1 4 1 3 1
1 4 1 3 1 3

Example 47

Example 47 uses the two notes which were used in the last example. This time the notes are used in conjunction with a bend. The third finger bends the string downwards towards the first string.

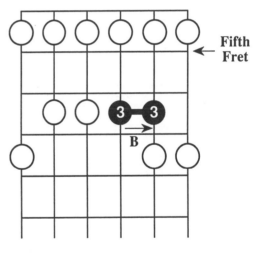

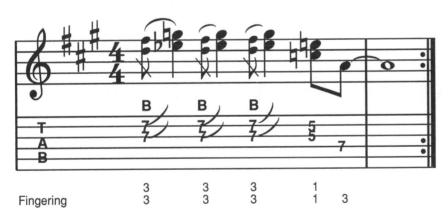

Fingering
3 3 3 1
3 3 3 1 3

Example 48

The final double-note lick introduces two notes played together on the second and third strings.

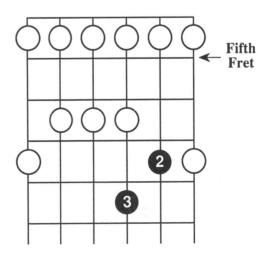

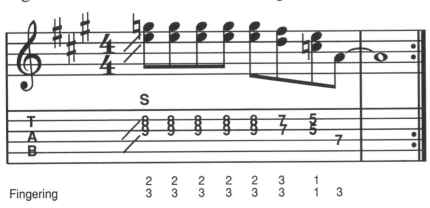

Fingering
2 2 2 2 2 3 1
3 3 3 3 3 3 1 3

Rock Guitar Solo 2
All For One And One For All

The second solo is played within pattern one and uses licks similar to the licks which have appeared earlier in the book. All the techniques discussed in previous lessons have also been incorporated into this solo. The chord progression chosen for this solo is a twelve bar blues progression in the key of G.

Twelve Bar Blues in G

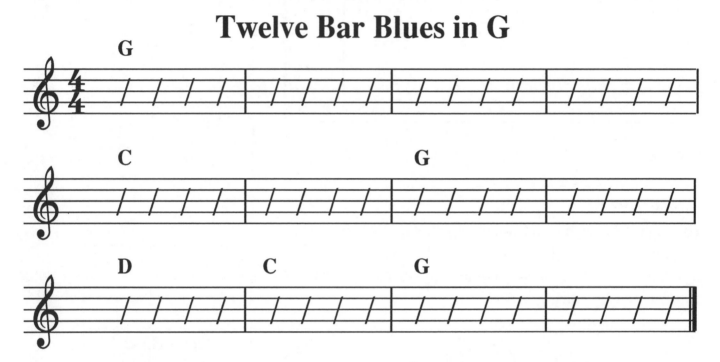

All For One And One For All – Analysis

• Hammers, pull-offs, slides and bends are used throughout the solo. These techniques were featured in Lessons 3 – 6.

• In the final bars of the solo, double note licks are played. This type of lick was explained in Lesson 8.

• Part of the Blues scale has been used for the solo in the final two bars. The blues scale was discussed in more detail in Lesson 7.

Create Your Own Solo

On the recording for this book the solo has been recorded on the right channel, and the drums, bass and rhythm guitar have been recorded on the left channel.

Once you can play this solo along with the backing track, try creating your own solo from licks you have learnt earlier in the book. Remember, all the licks will have to be played using pattern one at the third fret (in the key of G).

All For One And One For All

SECTION 2

Rock Guitar Licks
Pattern Two

Pattern Two

The next set of licks will be based upon the Minor Pentatonic scale within pattern two. This pattern may also be moved up or down the fretboard depending on which key is being used. As shown in the diagram below, the key notes are found on the second and fourth strings. Notice the location of pattern two in relation to pattern one. The key of G has been illustrated.

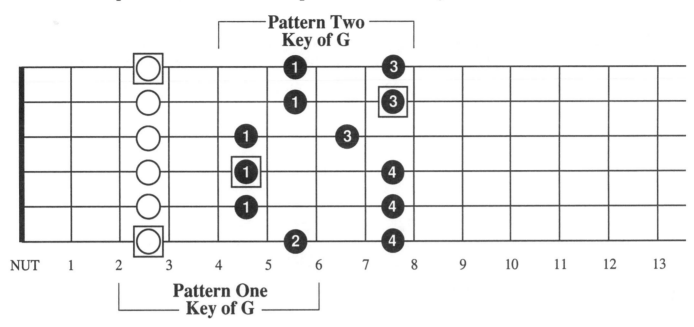

Example 49

The first example in this section ascends pattern two from the lowest note to the highest note. The example is played in the key of G, therefore corresponding with the above diagram.

Example 50

The next example descends pattern two from the highest note to the lowest note.

Lesson 9
Pattern Two – Key of G

As explained in the introduction to pattern two, the key of G is located between the fifth and eighth frets. The diagram below illustrates pattern two in the key of G. The key note (G), is on the second string. It will be essential to know all the notes on the second string to assist with playing pattern two in different keys. You will discover as you become comfortable with pattern two that the notes on the first three strings are most commonly used and these notes can be joined to pattern one. In fact, these notes are sometimes referred to as an extension of pattern one. The notes which are mainly used in pattern two are highlighted in the following diagram.

Fretboard Position

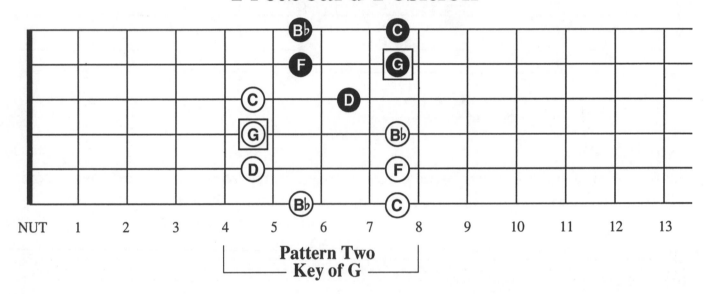

The Release Bend

Licks 52 - 55 feature pattern two in the key of G, as well as the use of the release bend. This technique is played by first bending the note indicated with the left hand, plucking the string whilst bent, then returning the string to its original position. The release bend creates a drop in pitch from a higher note to a lower note. A curved line on the top left hand side of the note and the letter R will indicate a release bend. The following example shows a release bend on the eighth fret of the first string.

Fingering   3

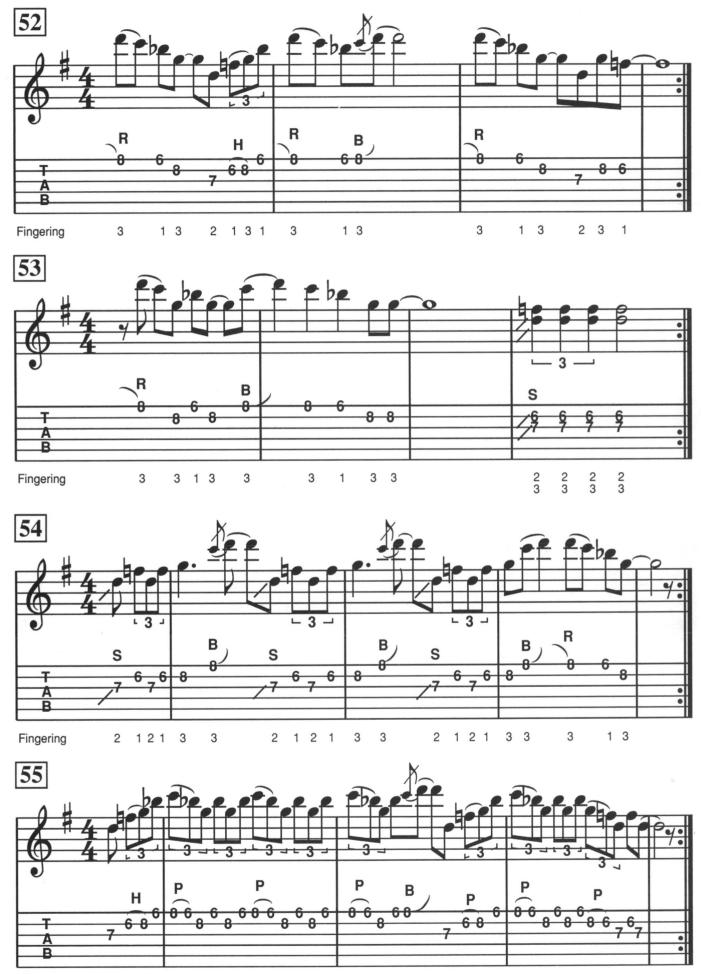

Lesson 10
Pattern Two - Key of F

As mentioned earlier, pattern two can be used as an extension of pattern one. The diagram below shows pattern one and the pattern one extension (pattern two) in the key of F.

Joining Patterns One and Two

The following examples show a popular way of changing from pattern one into pattern two, and back again. The change occurs on the third string with special attention given to the left hand fingering. The example shown is in the key of F.

Example 56

Fingering   1 4 1 3   1 3 1 3   3 1 3 1   3 1 3

Example 57

Fingering   3 1 3 1   3 1 1 3   1 3 1 4   1

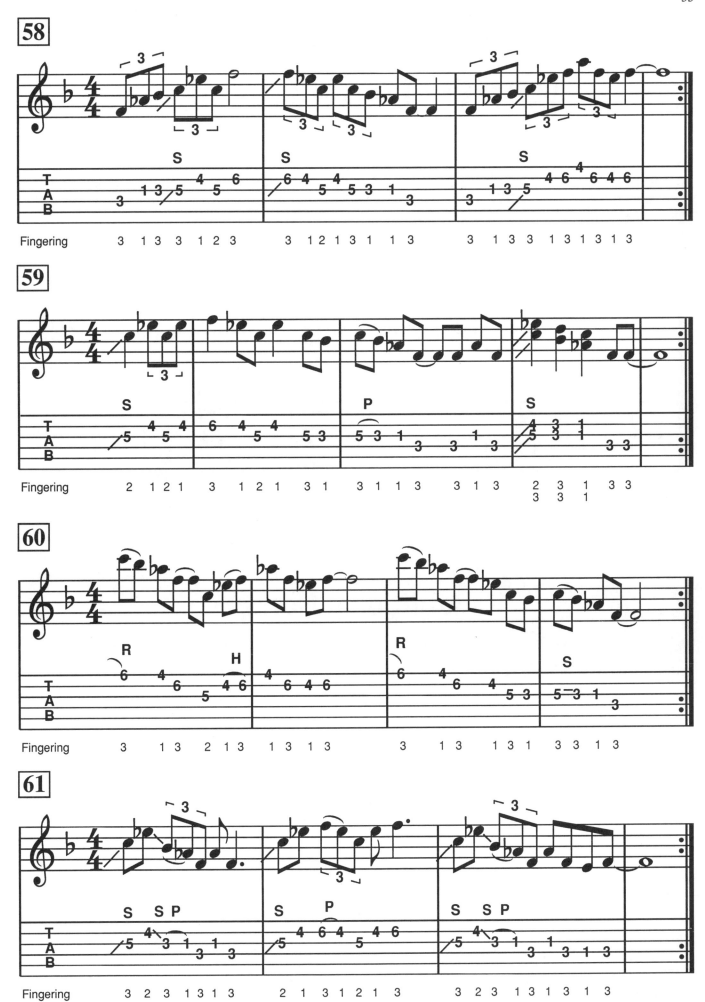

Lesson 11
Pattern Two – Key of C

The next lesson introduces pattern two in the key of C. The diagram below shows the fretboard position for pattern one, with the pattern one extension (pattern two) in the key of C.

Fretboard Position

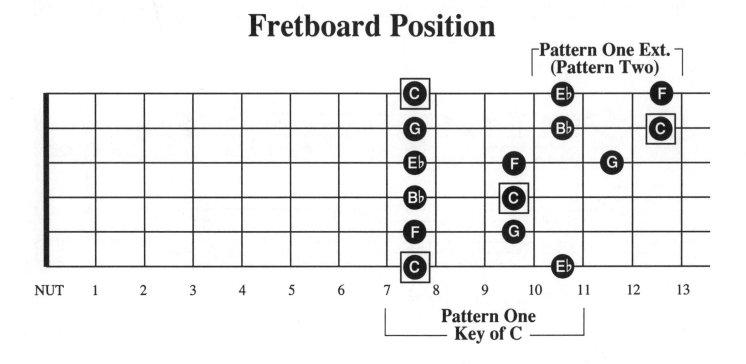

Additional Notes

The licks in this lesson will use an additional note in pattern one, and an additional note in pattern two. The additional note added in both patterns is the third note of the major scale. For example, the third note in the C Major scale (C D E F G A B C), is E. The diagram below shows the location of the extra note (E), when it is added to the C Minor Pentatonic scale (C E♭ F G B♭ C).

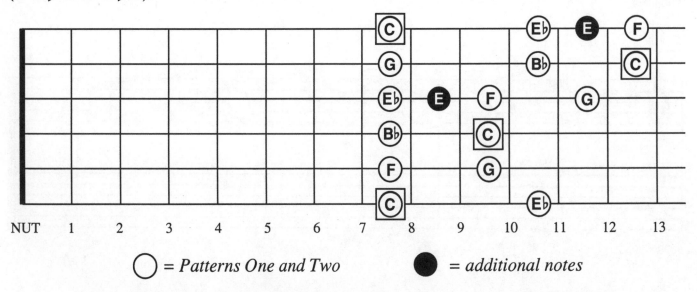

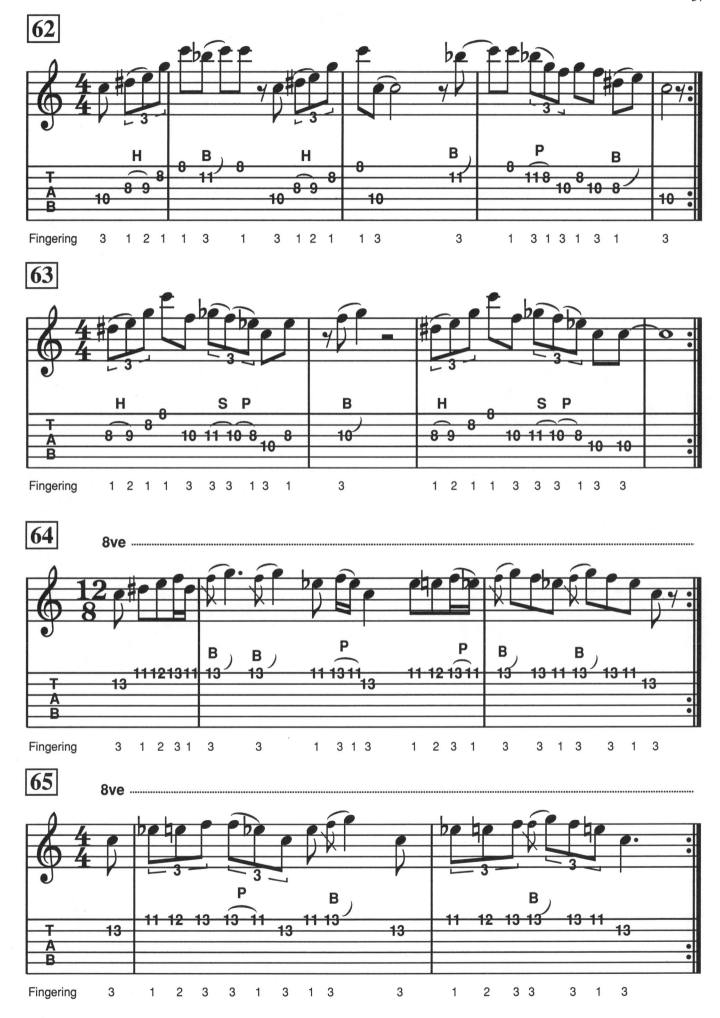

Lesson 12
Pattern Two – Key of A

Lesson twelve features the pattern one extension in the key of A, and also introduces additional notes which may be used in pattern one to create an alternative fingering. The diagram below shows the alternative fingering for pattern one with the pattern two extension. The example given is in the key of A. This optional fingering has been achieved by incorporating into the pattern, two additional notes on the fifth and sixth strings.

Fretboard Position - Alternative Fingering

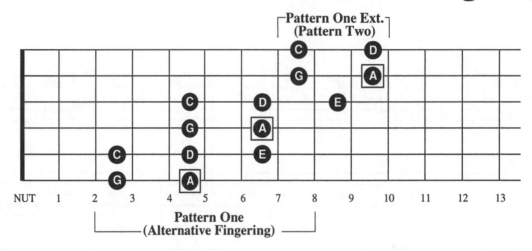

Now practice the following examples which ascend and descend the pattern using the alternative fingering. Attention should be given to the suggested fingering which is indicated below the tablature.

Example 66

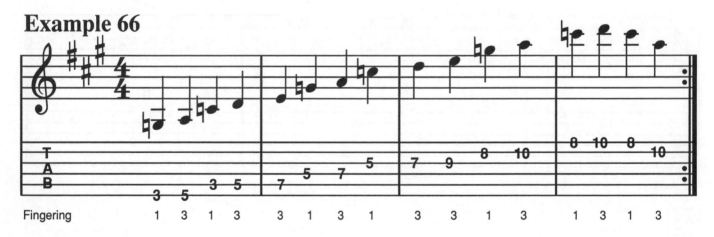

Example 67

Rock Guitar Solo 3
Two's Company

The third solo is played within pattern one and pattern two and uses licks similar to the ones which have appeared in the second section. All the techniques discussed in previous lessons have also been used in this solo. This solo is played over a blues-rock progression in the key of A. A $\frac{12}{8}$ rhythm is also used for this solo. This is a popular rhythm used in Blues and Rock consisting of 12 beats to the bar, divided into groups of three creating an accent every three beats.

Blues Rock Progression in A

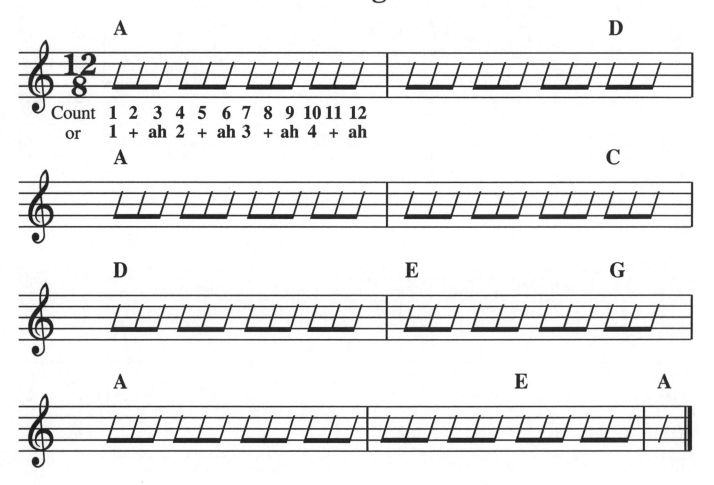

Two's Company – Analysis

- The opening four bars of the solo are played solely within pattern two. The additional note which may be added to pattern two (as explained in Lesson 11) has been used in the first bar. The release bend (Lesson 9) also appears in the first half of the solo.

- The solo moves to pattern one for the duration of the fifth and sixth bars.

- Double note licks complete the solo in bars seven and eight.

Two's Company

Patterns One and Two – Summary

Before continuing with the following lessons, revise the important points concerning pattern one and two as shown below. The structure of pattern one and two can be broken down into five steps.

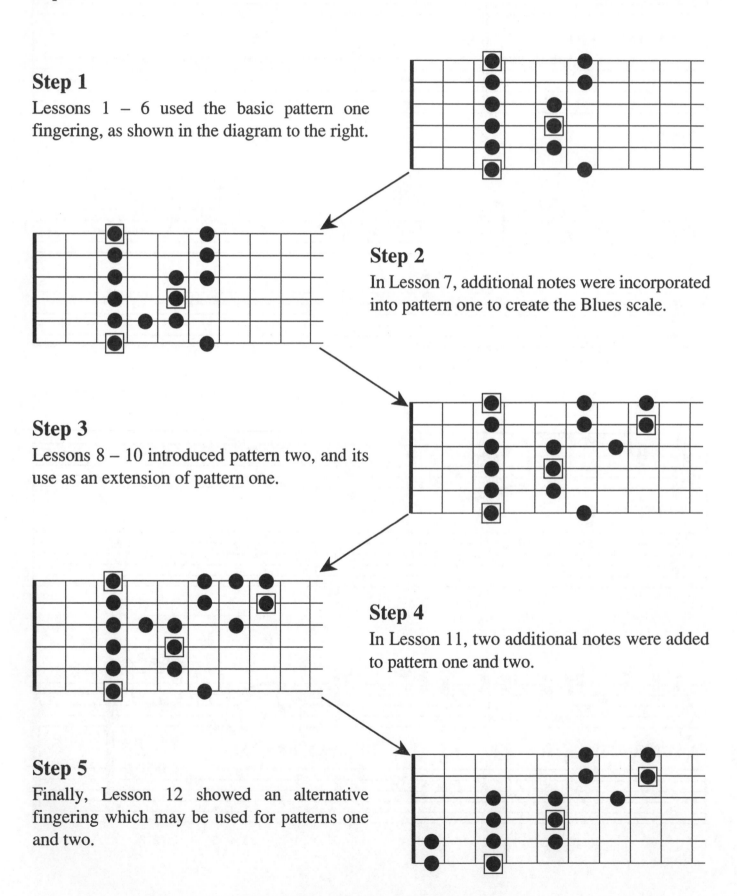

Step 1

Lessons 1 – 6 used the basic pattern one fingering, as shown in the diagram to the right.

Step 2

In Lesson 7, additional notes were incorporated into pattern one to create the Blues scale.

Step 3

Lessons 8 – 10 introduced pattern two, and its use as an extension of pattern one.

Step 4

In Lesson 11, two additional notes were added to pattern one and two.

Step 5

Finally, Lesson 12 showed an alternative fingering which may be used for patterns one and two.

SECTION 3

Rock Guitar Licks
Pattern Three

Pattern Three

The next section features rock guitar pattern number three. This pattern is found in a slightly higher position on the fretboard than pattern two.

The diagram below displays pattern three, and its position in relation to patterns one and two. The example given is in the key of G.

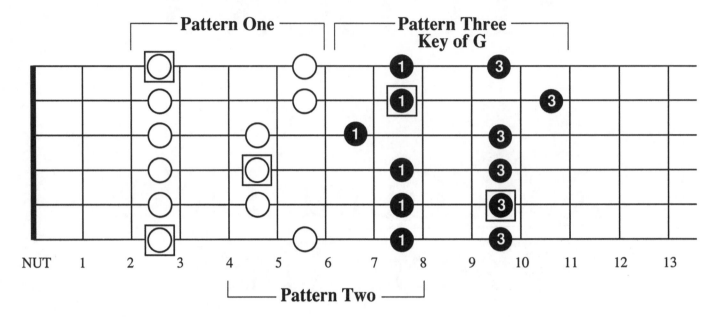

Practice the following examples which ascend and descend pattern three in the key of G.

Example 72

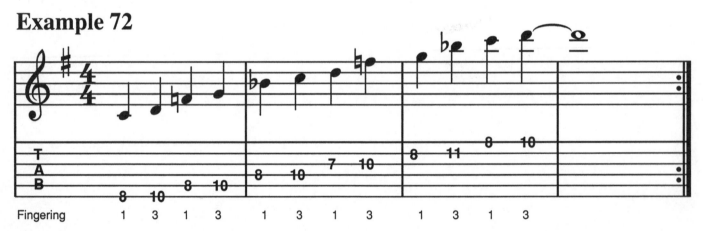

Example 73

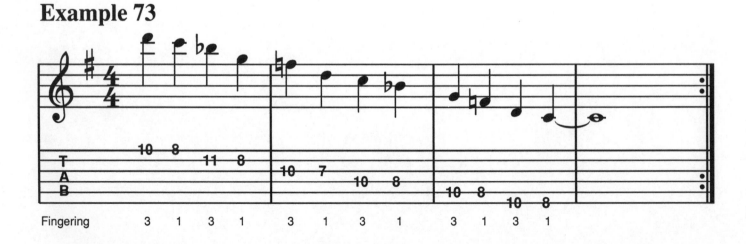

Pattern Three – The Blues Scale

As discussed in Lesson seven, an additional note may be added to the Minor Pentatonic scale to form the Blues scale. Therefore, this additional note may be added to pattern three. This note will not be used in pattern three as often as the other notes in the pattern, but when it is used it will help add a more "blues" like sound to your licks. The diagram below shows the three additional D♭ notes which may be added to pattern three to complete the Blues scale. The example given is in the key of G.

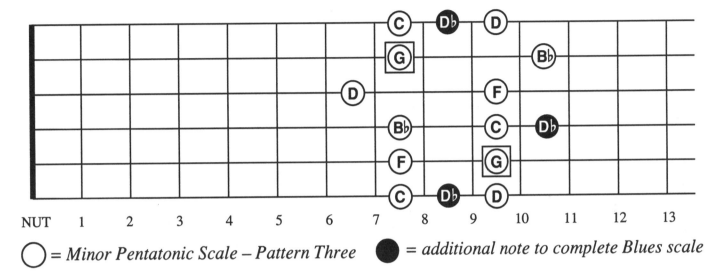

○ = *Minor Pentatonic Scale – Pattern Three* ● = *additional note to complete Blues scale*

Pattern Three – Additional Notes

As you will notice with the licks which will follow in this section, there are two more notes which may be added to pattern three. It is common practice to use additional notes on the third and second strings as shown in the diagram below.

These two notes are the second and sixth notes of the Major scale. As with the additional note to form the Blues scale, these notes are purely optional but when used in conjunction with the other notes in pattern three, will provide a more melodic "jazz" like sound.

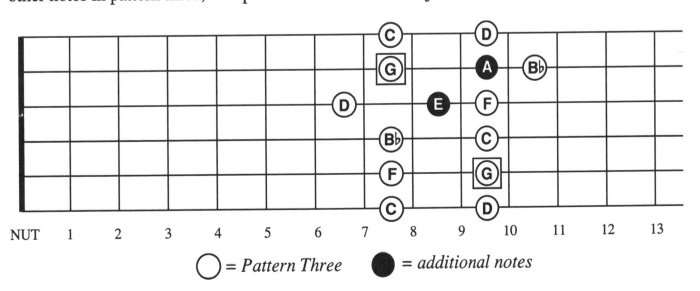

○ = *Pattern Three* ● = *additional notes*

Lesson 13
Pattern Three – Key of G

The next set of licks are played within pattern three in the key of G. The diagram below shows the fretboard position of pattern three in the key of G. The additional notes which may be used in the pattern, as explained in the introduction to pattern three, have also been shown.

Fretboard Position

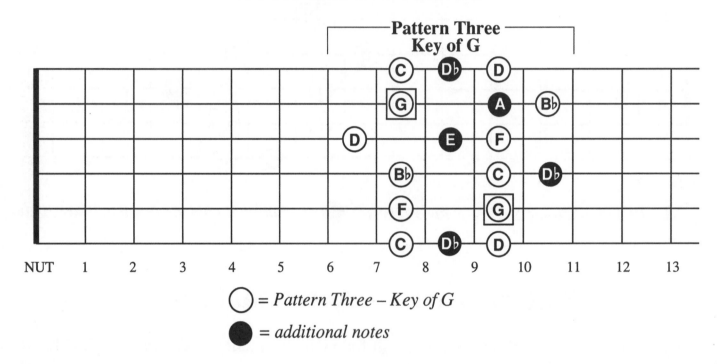

○ = *Pattern Three – Key of G*

● = *additional notes*

Vibrato

Licks 75 - 78 will also introduce the use of vibrato. Vibrato is controlled with the left hand finger which is fretting the note. As the finger frets the note, move the string rapidly back and forth in the direction of the adjacent strings. A wavy line shown above the tablature number indicates when vibrato is used.

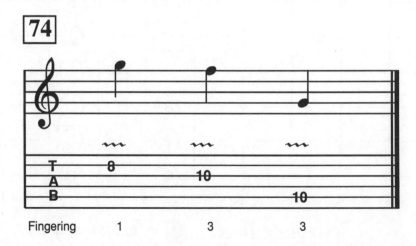

Lesson 14
Pattern Three – Key of B♭

The licks in Lesson 14 are played within pattern 3. This time the key of B♭ has been chosen. The diagram below shows the fretboard position for pattern 3 in the key of B♭. As with pattern two, you will find that the first three strings are mainly used in pattern three. It is still recommended that you memorize and practice all of the notes in pattern three, but as you become more familiar with this pattern you will find you will use the notes on the bass strings far less frequently than the notes found on the first three strings. The most commonly used notes in pattern three have been highlighted in the diagram below.

Fretboard Position

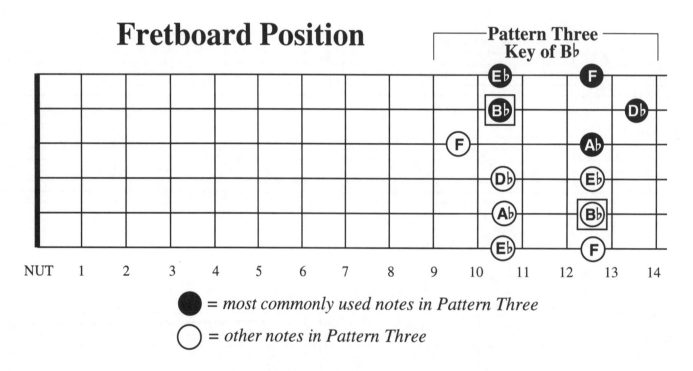

= *most commonly used notes in Pattern Three*

= *other notes in Pattern Three*

Double Note Licks

Licks 80 - 83 introduce another way of using a double note lick. This time a note is bent, and whilst the note is sustaining, another note is played with a different finger, causing both notes to ring together. The symbol ⌐‾‾‾⌐ is used in the tablature to show which two notes will ring together. In the following example, the 13th fret on the second string is bent with the third finger. As the note sustains, the fourth finger plays the note on the first string.

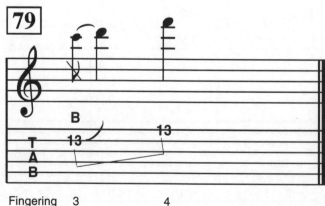

Lesson 15
Pattern Three – Key of C

Pattern three in the key of C is played between the 13th and 16th frets as shown in the diagram below. The following diagram also shows the position of pattern one and two in relation to pattern three. The licks in this lesson are played in the key of C and use all three patterns discussed so far.

Fretboard Position

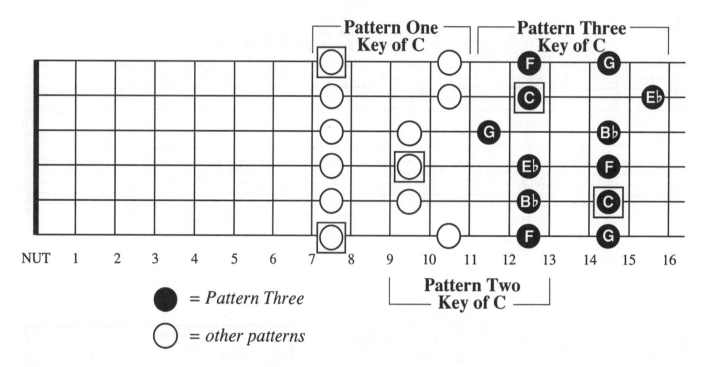

More Double Note Licks

Another popular technique used with double note licks is used in licks 86 - 89. This time two notes will be played simultaneously but only one note will be bent. This technique can be used in all patterns as shown in licks 85 - 88. In the following example both notes are played together, but only the third string is bent.

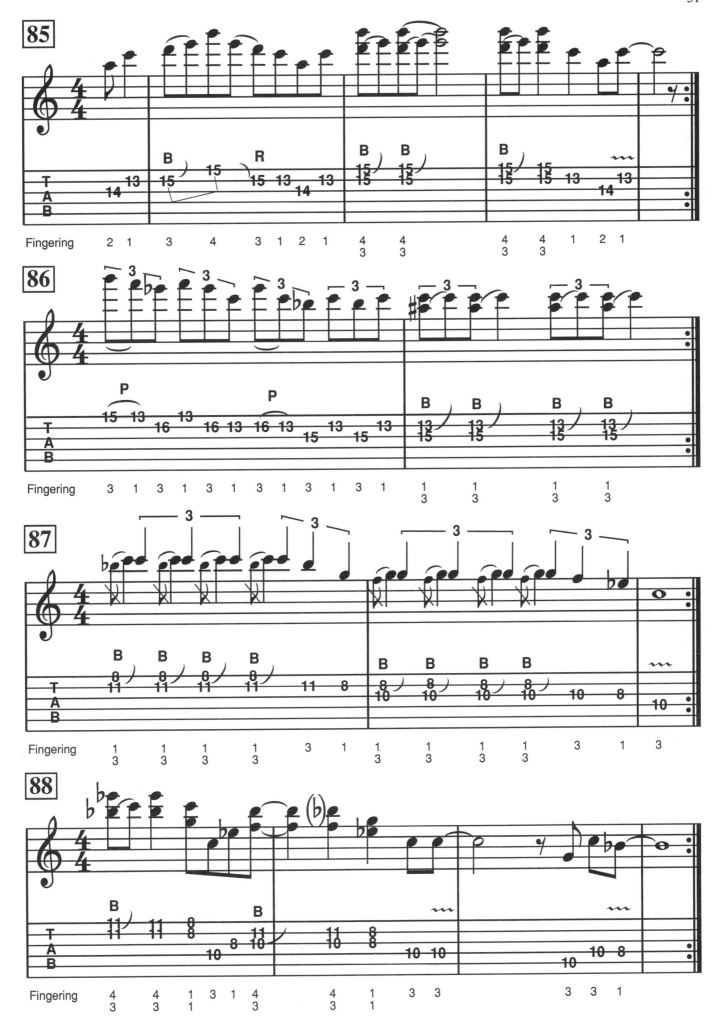

Rock Guitar Solo 4
The Hat-Trick

The fourth solo is in the key of C and uses all three patterns discussed so far. All the techniques used in recent lessons will also appear in this solo.

The solo is played over a jazz-blues progression in the key of C. The chord sequence is basically a 12 bar blues progression, but a "jazz" sound is created by the use of a "swing" rhythm. The swing rhythm is achieved by strumming a triplet rhythm (three strums to a beat), but only strumming the first and third part of the triplet. The rhythm is counted 1 ah 2 ah 3 ah 4 ah etc, as shown in the following chord chart.

Jazz – Blues Progression in C

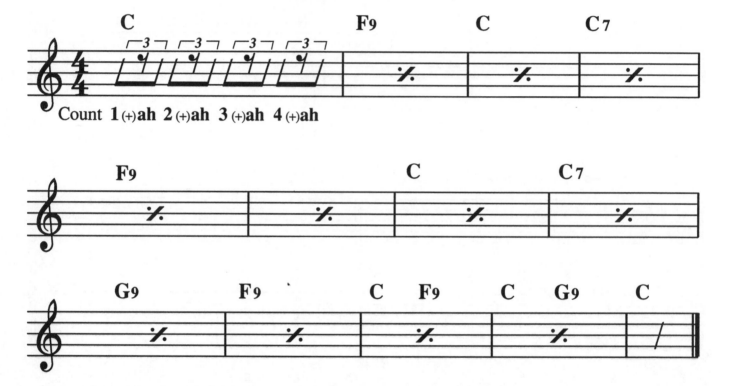

The Hat-Trick – Analysis

- The first half of this solo is played within pattern three. The additional notes which can be added to this pattern (as explained in the introduction to section 3) have been used also.

- Vibrato and double note licks are used throughout the solo. These techniques were discussed in lessons 13 and 14.

- The last half of this solo is played within patterns one and two.

The Hat-Trick

SECTION 4

Rock Guitar Licks
Pattern Four

Pattern Four

This section deals with lead guitar pattern number four. As with the other patterns discussed, this pattern is positioned slightly higher on the fretboard than pattern three. The diagram below shows pattern four, and its position on the fretboard in relation to patterns one, two and three. The example given is in the key of G.

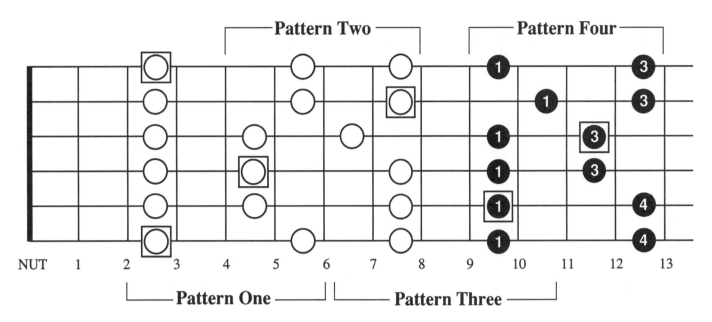

The following examples ascend and descend pattern four in the key of G.

Example 89

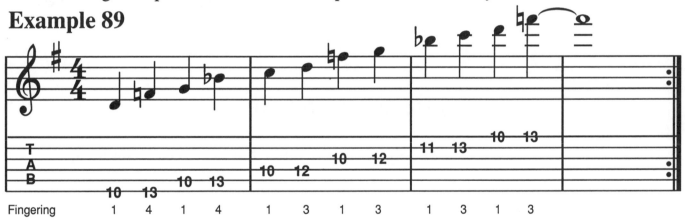

Example 90

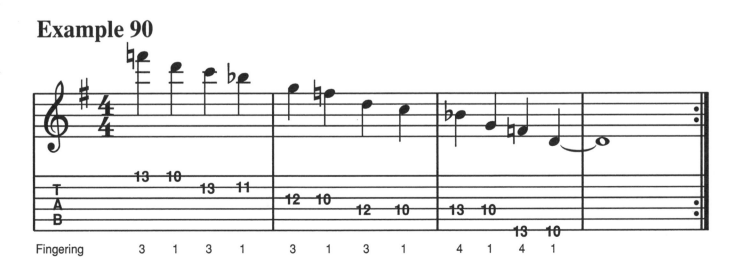

Lesson 16
Pattern Four – Key of G

Lesson Sixteen introduces pattern four in the key of G. Pattern Four in the key of G is positioned between the 10th and 13th frets as shown in the diagram below.

Fretboard Position

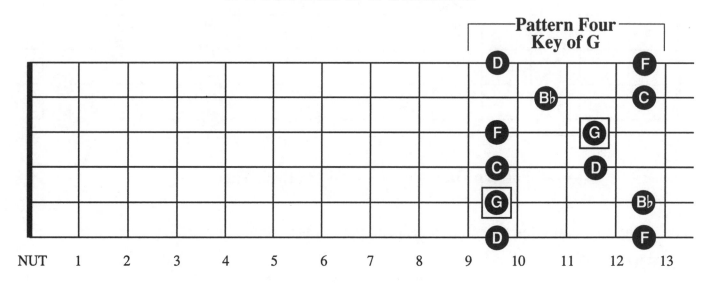

The Blues Scale

As with previous patterns, it will be helpful to know how the Blues scale can be applied to pattern four. This time the additional note to complete the Blues scale is on the second and fourth strings. The diagram below shows the additional note which may be added to pattern four to complete the Blues scale. The Blues scale has been used in licks 91 - 94.

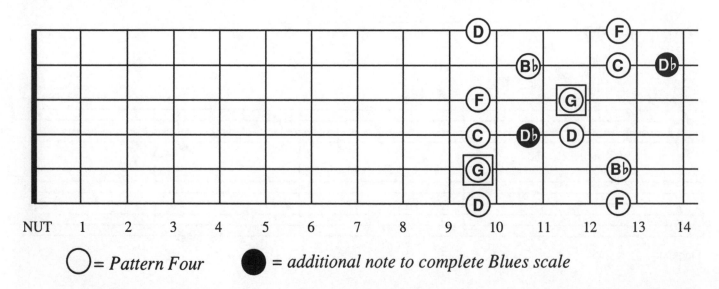

○ = Pattern Four   ● = additional note to complete Blues scale

Lesson 17
Pattern Four – Key of E

Lesson 17 will look at pattern four again but this time the key of E has been selected. Pattern four in the key of E is positioned between the seventh and tenth frets as shown in the diagram below. An alternative fingering for pattern four is also indicated in the following diagram. This fingering combines the notes found on the bass strings of pattern three with the treble strings of pattern four. Attention should be given to the location of the key notes and the additional note which may be added to the pattern to complete the blues scale.

Fretboard Position – Alternative Fingering

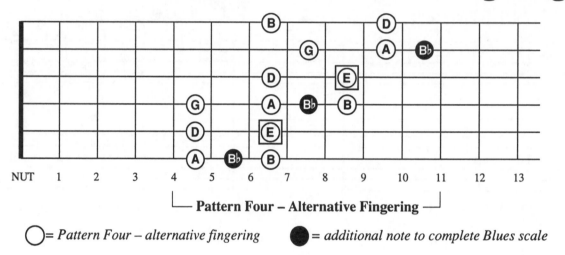

Pattern Four – Alternative Fingering

○ = *Pattern Four – alternative fingering*   ● = *additional note to complete Blues scale*

Practice the following examples which ascend and descend pattern four using the alternative fingering.

Example 95

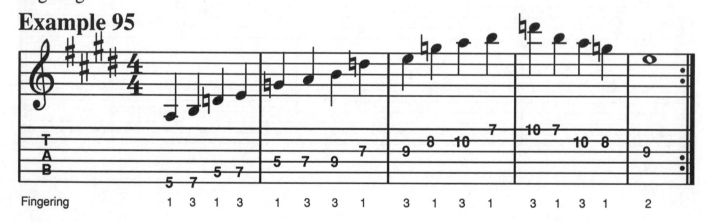

Example 96

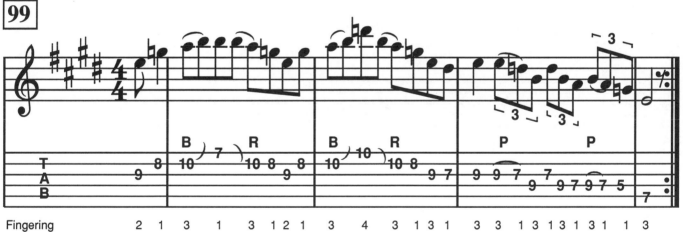

Rock Guitar Solo 5
The Fourth Dimension

Rock guitar solo number five is played in the key of E and only uses pattern four. This solo also features the use of the alternative fingering for pattern four which was discussed in Lesson seventeen. As you become more familiar with pattern four, you will find that this fingering is far more practical than the standard pattern four fingering shown in the introduction to section four. The chord sequence chosen for this solo is a rock progression in the key of E.

Rock Progression in E

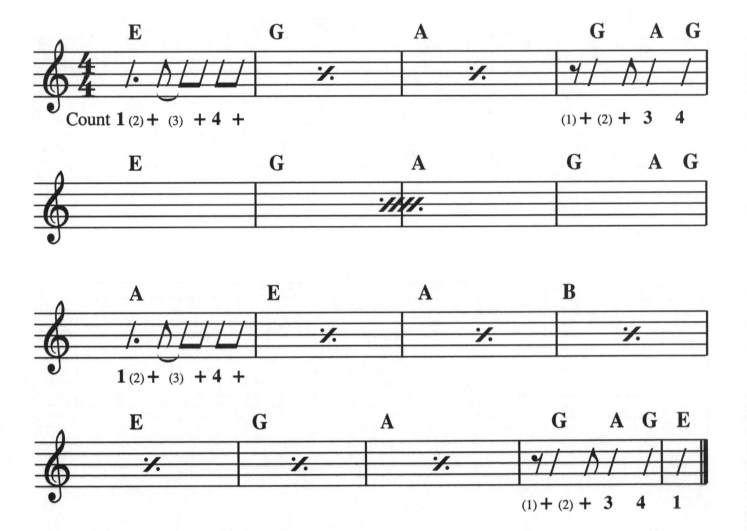

The Fourth Dimension – Analysis

- The entire solo is played within pattern four using the alternative fingering (as explained in Lesson 17).

- Special attention will need to be given to bar number 12. The first note in the bar (the ninth fret) is the only note struck with the right hand. The other notes are produced by hammering and pulling-off between the seventh and ninth frets with the first and third fingers of the left hand.

The Fourth Dimension

SECTION 5

Rock Guitar Licks
Pattern Five

Pattern Five

The final section shows lead guitar pattern number five. This pattern is positioned slightly higher on the fretboard than pattern four, as was the case with all patterns discussed previously. The diagram below illustrates pattern five, and its position on the fretboard in relation to patterns one, two, three and four. The example given is in the key of G.

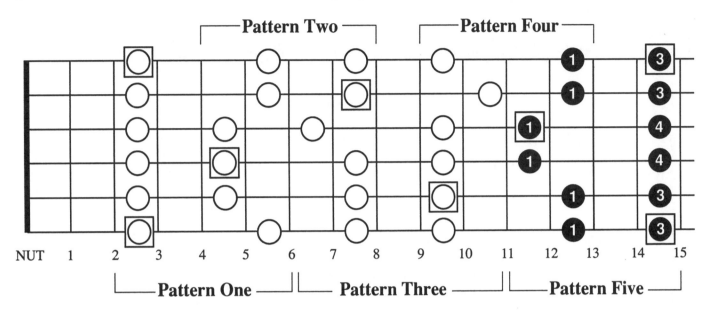

The following examples ascend and descend pattern five in the key of G.

Example 101

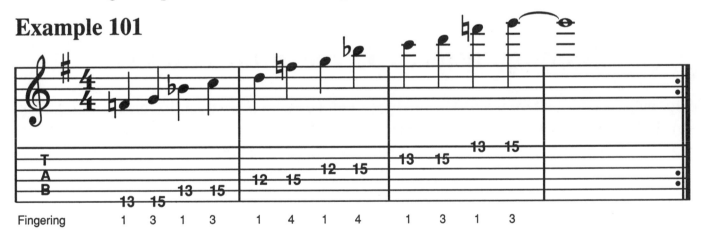

Example 102

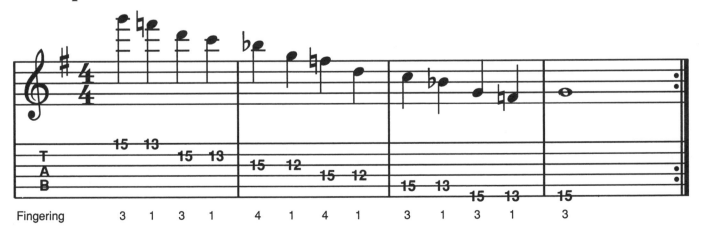

Lesson 18
Pattern Five – Key of G

The next set of licks will feature lead guitar pattern number five in the key of G. Although pattern five appears on all six strings, the notes found on the first and second strings are mainly used. The diagram below shows the fretboard position of pattern five in the key of G. The notes which have been highlighted are the notes which are mainly used within pattern five.

Fretboard Position

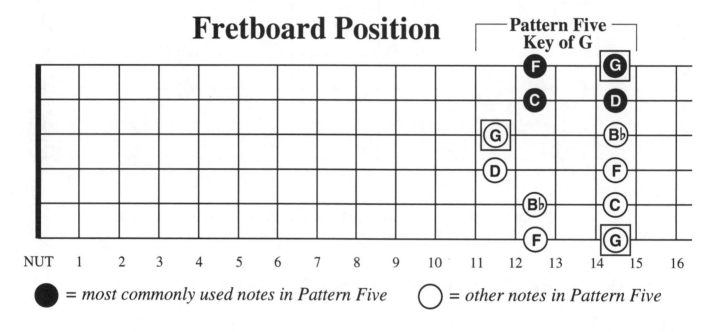

● = *most commonly used notes in Pattern Five* ○ = *other notes in Pattern Five*

Joining Patterns Three, Four and Five

A popular use for pattern five is to combine it with notes found in patterns three and four. This can be achieved in the following manner. In Lesson seventeen an alternative fingering for pattern four was discussed which utilized the bass strings of pattern three with the treble strings of pattern four. Add to this the notes on the first two strings from pattern five as explained above, and a comfortable pattern is obtained, moving in a diagonal manner from the bass notes of pattern three to the treble strings of pattern five. This new pattern is illustrated below.

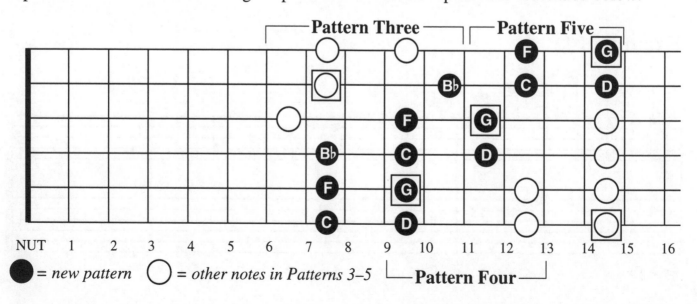

● = *new pattern* ○ = *other notes in Patterns 3–5*

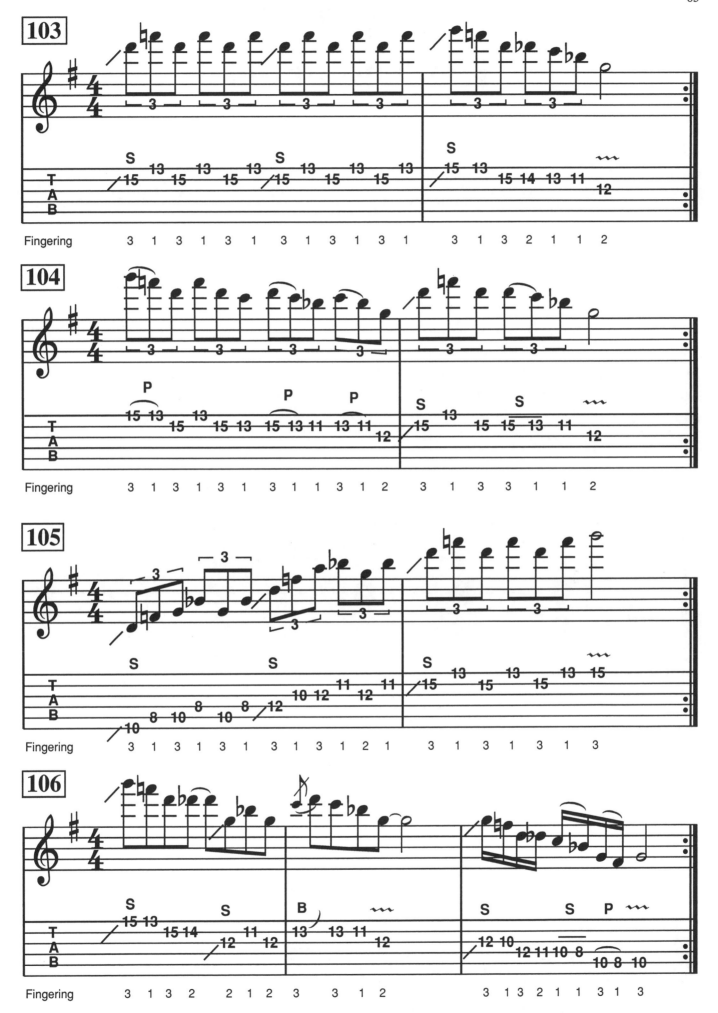

Rock Guitar Solo 6
The Pentathlon

Rock guitar solo number 6 is played in the key of D and uses patterns four and five in the same manner as explained in Lesson 18. Patterns four and five in the key of D are located between the third and tenth frets as shown in the diagram below.

Joining Pattern Five With Pattern One

Each time a new pattern has been introduced throughout this book, you will have noticed that its position on the fretboard is slightly higher than the previous pattern, i.e. pattern two is slightly higher on the fretboard than the previous pattern, pattern three is higher than pattern two, etc. The final thing to understand with patterns is that pattern five joins up with pattern one again, which joins up with pattern two again, etc. The location of pattern one in relation to pattern five has also been illustrated in the following diagram.

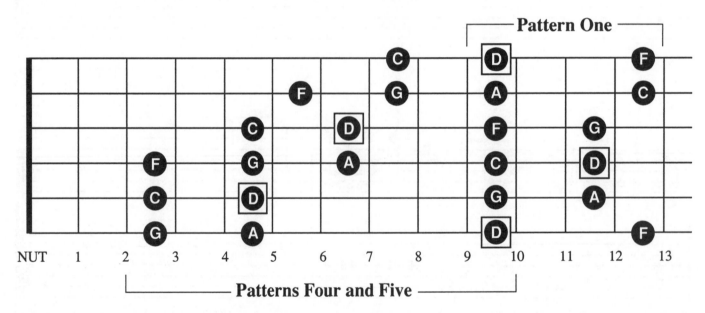

This time a common four bar Rock progression is repeated many times as the backing track for Rock Guitar Solo 6. This will give you the opportunity to create your own solo by playing along with the backing track as explained earlier, in the introduction to Rock Guitar solo 2.

Rock Progression in D

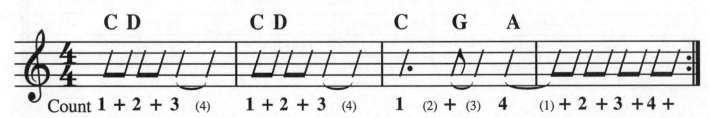

The Pentathlon

Patterns Three, Four and Five – Summary

The important points and practical uses of patterns three, four and five can be summarized in the following steps.

Step 1

Lessons 13 – 15 discussed the uses of pattern three, with the inclusion of additional notes and Blues notes.

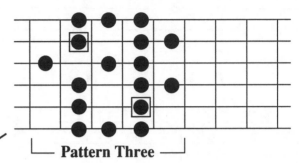

Pattern Three

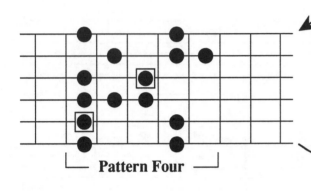

Pattern Four

Step 2

Lesson 16 showed pattern four and the additional notes which may be added to pattern four to complete the Blues scale.

Step 3

An alternative fingering combining patterns three and four was detailed in Lesson 17.

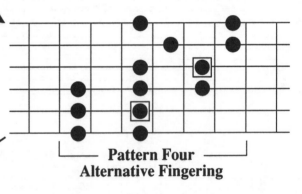

Pattern Four
Alternative Fingering

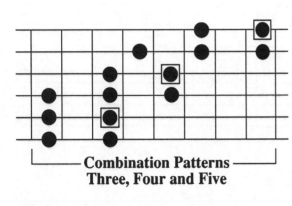

Combination Patterns
Three, Four and Five

Step 4

A new pattern derived from all three patterns featured in Lesson 18.

Step 5

Finally, the joining of pattern five and pattern one was incorporated into Rock Guitar Solo number 6.

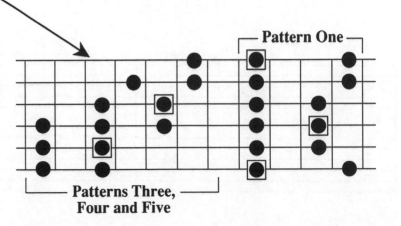

Pattern One

Patterns Three,
Four and Five

SECTION 6

Fretboard
Diagrams

The following fretboard diagrams highlight rock guitar patterns one to five in all keys.

Key of A

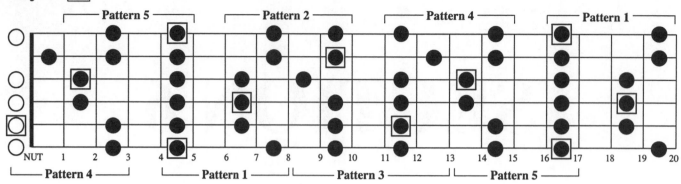

Key of A♯/B♭

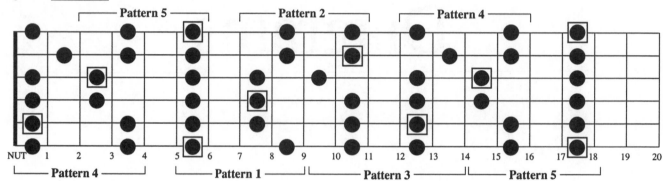

Key of B

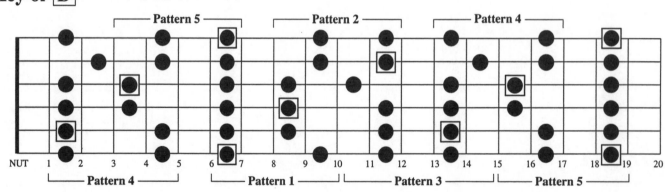

Key of C

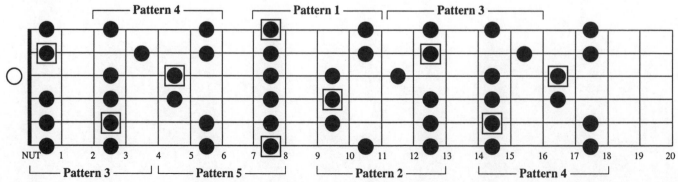

Key of C♯/D♭

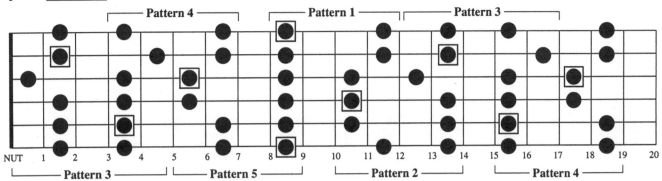

Key of D

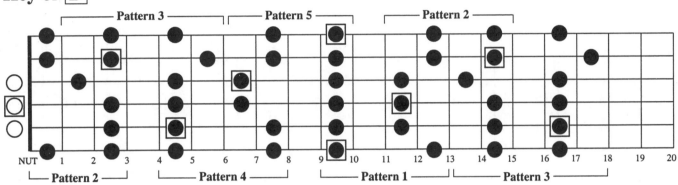

Key of D♯/E♭

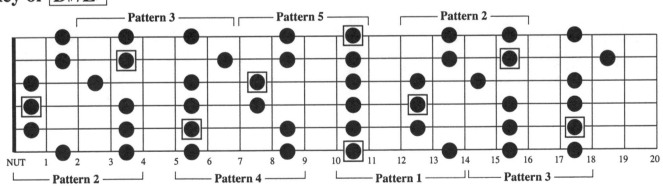

Key of E

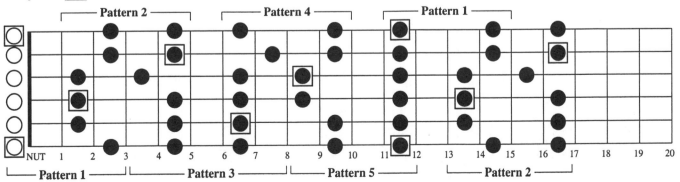

72

Key of F

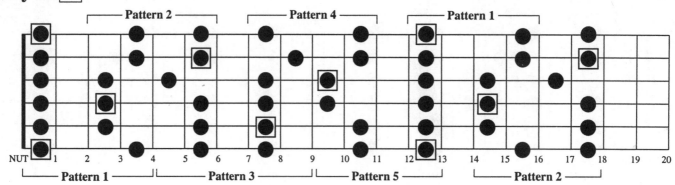

Key of F♯/G♭

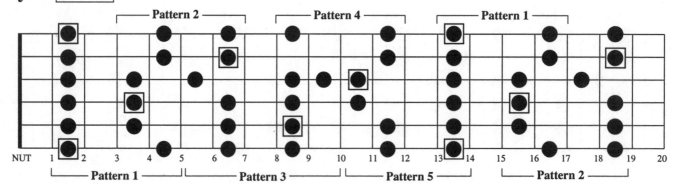

Key of G

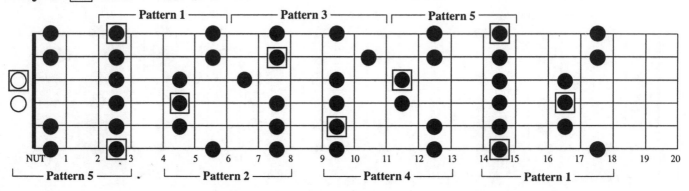

Key of G♯/A♭

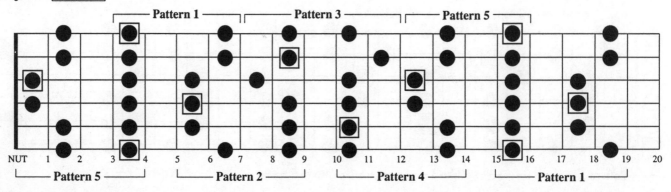